KU-369-970

Books should be returned or renewed by the last
date above. Renew by phone **03000 41 31 31** or
online *www.kent.gov.uk/libs*

Libraries Registration & Archives

MYSTERIES

OF THE

CONSTELLATIONS

by Lela Nargi

Raintree is an imprint of Capstone Global Library Limited, a company incorporated in England and Wales having its registered office at 264 Banbury Road, Oxford, OX2 7DY – Registered company number: 6695582

www.raintree.co.uk
myorders@raintree.co.uk

Edited by Hank Musolf
Designed by Sara Radka
Original illustrations © Capstone Global Library Limited 2021
Picture research by Jo Miller
Production by Laura Manthe
Originated by Capstone Global Library Ltd
Printed and bound in India

978 1 3982 0477 5 (hardback)
978 1 3982 0476 8 (paperback)

British Library Cataloguing in Publication Data
A full catalogue record for this book is available from the British Library.

Acknowledgements
We would like to thank the following for permission to reproduce photographs: Alamy: Science History Images, 16; International Astronomical Union: M. Zamani, 22; iStockphoto: libre de droit, 21, TOLGA DOGAN, 11; Newscom: World History Archive, 12 (Inset); Science Source: Chris Butler, 25, David A. Hardy, 19, Jerry Lodriguss, 28, Larry Landolfi, 9 (Bottom), TIM BROWN, 17, Tim Vernon, 29; Shutterstock: Genevieve de Messieres, 27, Josep.Ng, 13, KoSSSmoSSS, 7, M Andy, 9 (Top), Martina Badini, 5, Masahiro Suzuki, 8, oxameel, 14, shooarts, 24, Taeya18, Cover, thipjang, 6; U.S. Navy: photo by Mass Communication Specialist Seaman Michele Fink, 10. Design elements: Shutterstock: Anna Kutukova, Aygun Ali

CONTENTS

Words in **bold** are in the glossary.

CHAPTER 1

SHAPES ABOVE

The night is clear. You can see the stars. Some of the stars form patterns and shapes. The Plough and Orion are two of the most famous constellations.

Constellations help us make sense of the night sky. They can be used to guide people who are travelling. They allow us to keep track of time. But who discovered them? How do people use constellations to guess the future? How do astronomers use constellations? What mysteries of space can be solved by studying these star patterns?

Lascaux cave paintings

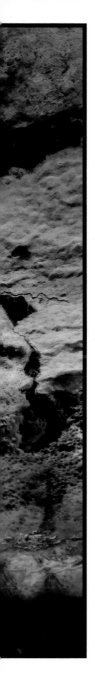

SEEING STAR PATTERNS

People have looked for patterns of stars in the sky for a long time. Different cultures throughout history found different shapes. A 17,000-year-old cave painting in France shows a rhinoceros constellation. A 6,000-year-old tomb in China held drawings of dragon and tiger constellations. The Mayans filled books with turtle, bat and frog star shapes.

SAME STARS, DIFFERENT NAMES

Some cultures had different names for the same star groups. The Corona Borealis is also called the Northern Crown. Ursa Major is often called The Great Bear.

CHAPTER 2

WHAT'S IN A PICTURE?

Constellations are fun to spot in the sky. But they are also tools. Before calendars, people looked at stars to help them know when seasons would change. When Scorpio got two extra tail stars in spring, it was time to plant crops.

Stars of Orion

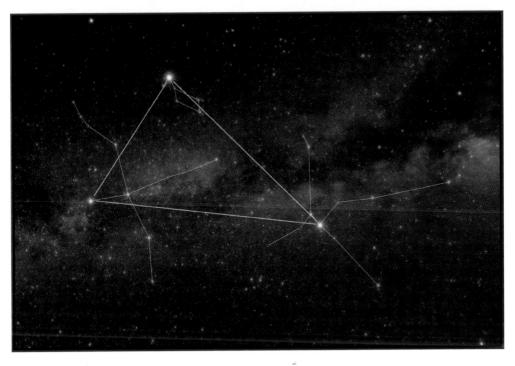

Summer Triangle

The Summer Triangle meant it was time to harvest crops. Winter was near when Orion appeared. The stars helped farmers to plan out their fields in good time. Some farmers still know these signs.

Orion

FINDING OUR WAY

Ship's crews once used stars to find their way at sea. Sailors looked for the constellations called the Plough and Cassiopeia. This helped them to find the star Polaris. Polaris is between the Plough and Cassiopeia. It is always in the north. That is why it is also called the North Star. By finding it, sailors would know which direction they were going. Navies still teach sailors how to use **celestial** navigation.

A sextant uses the distance between its user and the stars to help sailors navigate.

Birds use stars and the
Moon for navigation.

CHAPTER 3

ANCIENT STARGAZING

Around 1200 BC, Babylonians and Sumerians mapped many constellations. They passed their knowledge to the Romans and Greeks. A scientist from anicent Greece called Ptolemy wrote a book in AD 150. It named 48 constellations.

Twelve of the constellations were **zodiac** constellations. The ancient Greeks and others thought the zodiac told the future. People today still read zodiac predictions. Your zodiac sign is based on the day you were born.

Ptolemy

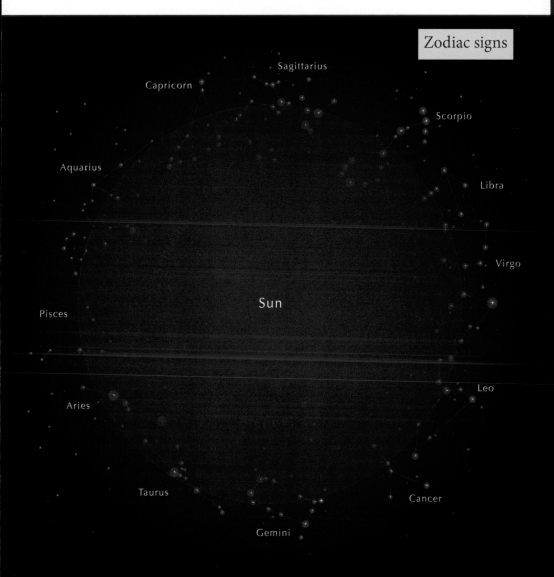

Sagittarius

Capricorn

Scorpio

Aquarius

Libra

Virgo

Sun

Pisces

Leo

Aries

Taurus

Cancer

Gemini

MYSTERY FACT

The belief that we can tell the future
from stars is called **astrology**.

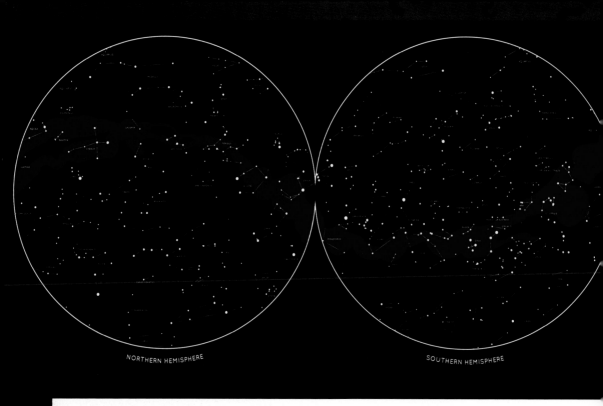

NORTHERN HEMISPHERE

SOUTHERN HEMISPHERE

MAPPING THE SOUTHERN SKY

Some early **astronomers** lived in the northern **hemisphere**. They could only see northern stars, so they only mapped northern constellations. Northern people started to sail to the southern hemisphere in the 1550s. Aboriginal people already knew the stars there. Now northern people got their first look.

CONSTELLATIONS

Some astronomers named constellations after kings. An English scientist named 13 constellations after toads, leeches and slugs. None of these names stuck!

Discoveries are being made within the constellations today. Scientists discovered a black hole within Sagittarius. A **black hole** is a part of space with strong gravity that pulls in anything that comes close.

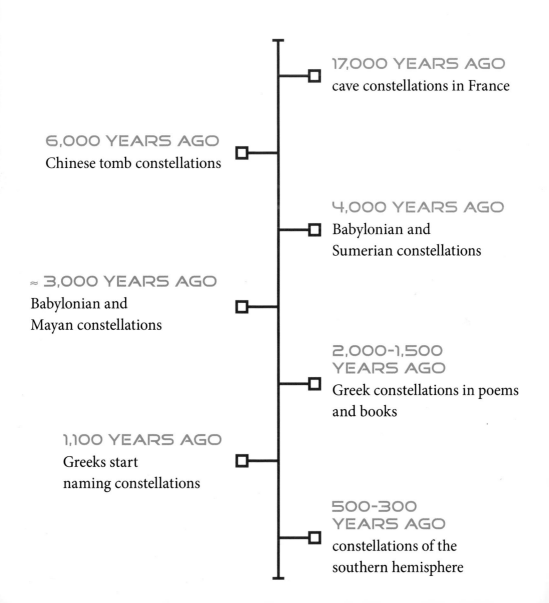

17,000 YEARS AGO
cave constellations in France

6,000 YEARS AGO
Chinese tomb constellations

4,000 YEARS AGO
Babylonian and Sumerian constellations

≈ 3,000 YEARS AGO
Babylonian and Mayan constellations

2,000-1,500 YEARS AGO
Greek constellations in poems and books

1,100 YEARS AGO
Greeks start naming constellations

500-300 YEARS AGO
constellations of the southern hemisphere

CHAPTER 4

HOW CONSTELLATIONS "MOVE"

It looks like stars in constellations move. What we really see is Earth moving.

Our planet spins on its **axis**. One spin equals one day. Earth passes constellations as it spins. They seem to rise and set.

Our planet **orbits** the Sun. One orbit equals one year. Different constellations come into view as we make this journey.

A **planisphere** is a wheel that helps locate constellations.

A celestial sphere is an imaginary sphere where constellations can be seen.

Some constellations are visible every night. Others only appear on some nights. Scientists know which constellations will appear each night. They make maps of the sky that show which constellations you'll be able to see based on the time of year and your location.

CHAPTER 5

LOOKING DEEPER

The universe is expanding. Objects in space pull away from each other.

So stars do move, and constellations change shape. But we do not notice because the changes take hundreds of years.

Earth wobbles as it spins. This means seasons shift over time. We see the zodiac at different times now.

Let's go back 5,000 years. Spring came when the Sun passed through Taurus. Now it comes when the Sun passes through Pisces.

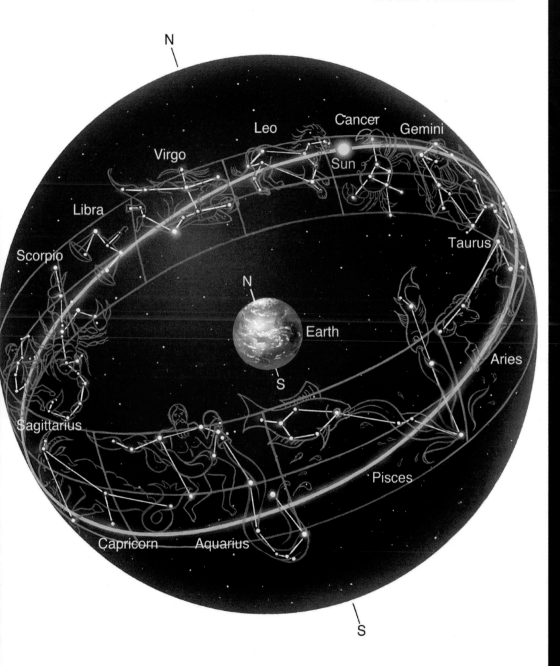

CONSTELLATION VS ASTERISM

Some sky shapes are **asterisms**. Asterisms may have fewer stars than constellations. They have names, but astronomers do not officially recognize them.

An asterism may be part of a constellation. An example is the Plough. It is part of the Great Bear constellation. The Northern Cross asterism is part of the Cygnus constellation.

Some asterisms span constellations. The Summer Triangle is made up of three stars. Deneb is in Cygnus. Vega is in Lyra. Altair is in Aquila.

MYSTERY FACT

Other names for the Plough:
- The Big Dipper, United States
- The Saucepan, France
- An Emperor's Chariot, China
- Ursa Major

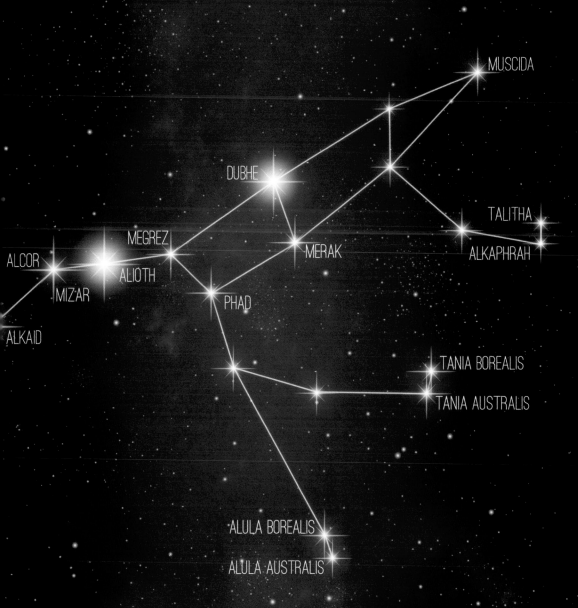

URSA MAJOR
THE GREAT BEAR

MUSCIDA

DUBHE

TALITHA

ALKAPHRAH

MEGREZ

MERAK

ALCOR

ALIOTH

MIZAR

PHAD

ALKAID

TANIA BOREALIS

TANIA AUSTRALIS

ALULA BOREALIS

ALULA AUSTRALIS

IT'S OFFICIAL

What makes a constellation official? The International Astronomical Union, or IAU, decides. The IAU is a group of astronomers. They name stars and explain the sky. They took 48 northern hemisphere constellations. They broke them into 50 constellations. They added 38 southern hemisphere constellations.

These are our 88 official constellations. We can see 60 in each hemisphere. We never see more than 24 at a time. The IAU calls every other star shape an asterism.

The members of the IAU vote to make decisions about constellations.

CHAPTER 6

COUNTRIES IN THE SKY

As we have seen, IAU divided the sky into 88 pieces. They named each piece after its constellation.

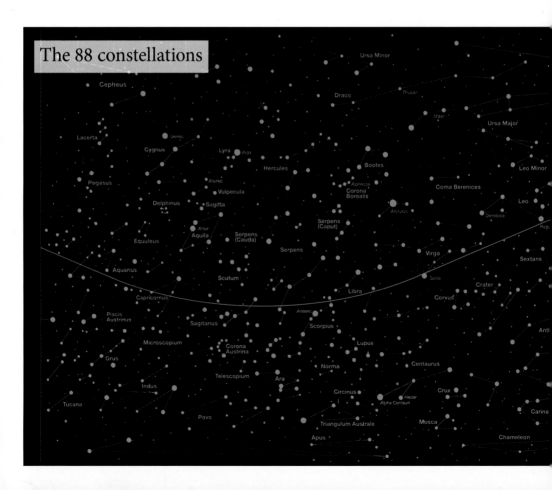

The 88 constellations

Imagine the 88 sky pieces are countries. Each country has borders. Inside its borders lies one constellation. The country is named after it. Orion, Leo, the Giraffe and Draco are some constellation countries.

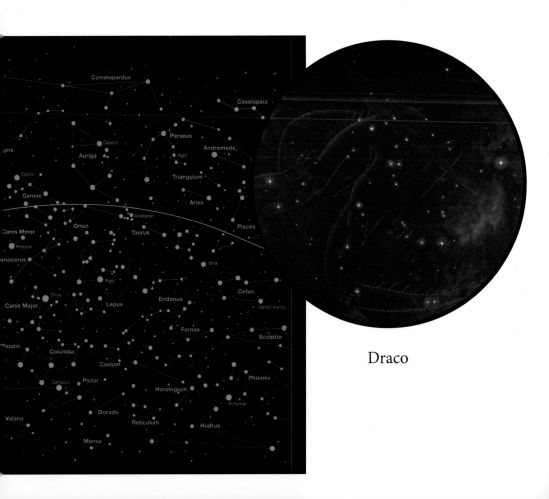

Draco

A JOB FOR CONSTELLATIONS

Constellations once had a job. People used to rely on them to navigate. Calendars and navigating tools took over. We stopped using astrology as science. The IAU gave constellations a job again.

We first named stars we could see with our eyes. Then we invented telescopes. We could see even more stars. Now we find new stars all the time. We need an easy way to tell people where old and new stars are.

A star takes part of its name from its constellation. It takes part of its name from its brightness. Alpha is brightest. Omega is the least bright. The brightest star in Taurus is called Alpha Tauri.

MYSTERY FACT

Stars in a constellation are not the same distance from one another. Bright stars may be further away than dim stars.

Taurus and the Pleiades
star cluster

CHAPTER 7

OLD IS NEW

Astronomers once used words from their own cultures to name constellations. **Archeoastronomers** study ancient sky cultures.

The IAU gives ancient names to some stars. Four stars now have Aboriginal names. And 86 stars now have Chinese, Hindu, Mayan and Polynesian names. Astronomers continue to look for new discoveries wtihin constellations, such as new black holes. They use advanced telescopes and other tools as they study the sky. What do you think they might find next?

Canis Major, the "Big Dog".

El Caracol Observatory helped the ancient Mayans study the stars to help with farming.

GLOSSARY

archeoastronomer scientist who studies the astronomical knowledge of ancient people

asterism small group of stars within a larger constellation

astrology study of how the positions of the stars and planets affect people's lives

astronomer scientist who studies stars, planets and other objects in space

axis line that runs through the centre of Earth; Earth spins around it

black hole invisible region of space with a strong gravitational field

celestial relating to the stars and the sky

hemisphere one half of Earth; the equator divides Earth into northern and southern hemispheres

orbit travel around an object in space; an orbit is also the path an object follows while circling an object in space

planisphere sky map that allows you to see which constellations will be overhead at night

zodiac twelve constellations through which the Sun, moons and planets move each month

FIND OUT MORE

BOOKS

The Mysteries of the Universe: Discover the best-kept secrets of space, DK (DK Children, 2020)

StarFinder for Beginners, DK (DK Children, 2017)

Women Scientists in Astronomy and Space (Superwomen in STEM), Nancy Dickmann (Raintree, 2020)

WEBSITES

www.bbc.co.uk/bitesize/topics/zdrrd2p
Discover more about the solar system.

www.dkfindout.com/uk/space/constellations
Find out more about constellations.

www.esa.int/kids/en/home
Learn more about space from the European Space Agency.

INDEX